BETTING

On

YOUR

BABY

∞ ∞ ∞

JAMIE SHAW

SWEETSPIRE LITERATURE
—— MANAGEMENT ——

HOW
the
PETALS
SHIVER

∞ ∞ ∞

New Dew & Sunlight *unto thee*

To feel Sun, in ages won,
I gather up my tears
A lover smothers, born to bundle
Incremental peers
In time, to neither grieve *adieu*,
Nor, eons yet to come,
Believe in ciao's *tiramisu—*
A pick-me-up too rum
To save *Carina* from a smarting
Innocent regret:
For, in her eyes, my soul (apart
From babes on whom I bet)

Is what a thorn is to her rose—
New dew and sunlight, comatose!

HOW *the PETALS* SHIVER

One

When five-point-eight millennia
Configurate my heart,
Temptations baiting many a
Prognosticator chart
The Devil in the detail's
Artfulness in art—
My *femme fatale* a female's
Pin to pull apart!
In love? My lover's loving *not*—
A snigger's convoluting
Victory to govern what
Her figure's got, refuting
The wreck I am: I trek, inspecting
Catacombs within
This tissue scarr'd they want injecting
Stabilizers in—
Arthurian a King, a Knight
For Guinevere, in lieu
Of leading lights her legend might
Less posthumously rue!

THE LEOPARD

Two

In corridors he paces, free
From foraging for food;
Through sombre eyes a little sea
Is hard to notice, view'd

By all and sundry, keen to pay
Lip-service to the light
Within a soul, whose ev'ry *trait*
Is gold, and black, and white...

If he could stretch his legs, and leap
Beyond the wire doors,
To find a place where hopes are deep
In antelope his jaws

Devour slowly—maybe, then,
He should consider bones
Not wholly the domain of men
With hearts of tin, and stones.

LITTLE FRIEND

Three

She opens beatific eyes
I gingerly oppose
With sea-blue green—'tis no surprise
Each other chose a rose

To be a friend till, at the end
Of nettlesome degrees,
Our petals start to shiver, sending
Fettle on the breeze...

But time for rhyme is up and gone—
Togetherness apart
Must flourish, where, in Avalon,
Will break tomorrow's heart:

O Brother, Friend, O Lancelot,
Be kind, envelop her
In amity's intrepid knot
We tether—lest she stir.

ON PIANO, IN A HEAD

four

A tom to trump all kitties,
Whether white or ginger-red,
Conglomerating ditties
On piano, in a head
Fraternity so pities—
Left to wonder: Will they wed
Bits of eloquence to wit, these
Moggie aspirants to cred!

Let remain the true believers
Whosoever would dethrone
Pretenders come to grieve *hers*—
If *Our Puss* should e'er bemoan
Bent blackguards, brats, or bullies
Come contending to displace
Liege lover cats, be cool, seize
Dumb deciduous each case!

YESTER EVE

five

In craving an allegiance, where
A better hadn't been,
She ping'd an answer, to ensnare
My Kingdom for a Queen!
I drifted off, to sponsor sleep,
But royalty remain'd
Ensconced in my subconscious deep—
Or so to do it deign'd...
What follows is for covert eyes—
Sequester only *mine*
I should, except (I realize)
I am annexing *thine*:
The regent, of whom many years
Be thinking with a smile,
Made love to me, as winter clears
For summer's country mile...
And oh, such love, a love supreme,
How can it not be true?
To sense it, feel it in a dream—
And then, to think of *you*!

DREAM SHIVA

Six

Destroyer God—she's going well,
As well as gods can go—
If she could be my solar cell,
Fluorescent inner glow,
My windmill in her summer breeze,
My stitch-in-time to sew,
I'd fall before her, on my knees,
Thank Heavens, then bestow—
No raiments, gold, no frankincense,
No temporary myrrh,
For just to catch a whiff of whence
Her transcendental purr
Came from on high, to grace this board
We're playing on—*the Earth*—
Were my reward, for one outlaw'd
She's won by winsome worth,
Sees loss to boss in royal games,
Lest, breaking up like glass,
I must resign, as Shiva tames
Me—seeing through her class!

CRUSH

Seven

Upon a bench there sat a fly
As motionless as gold—
As easily to vilify
As anti-social mould:
How ever came this monster mean
To populate the air
I call my own? Where it has been
To think of doesn't bear...
No devil knew how great its guile,
Foiling ev'ry plot
Of man, or mouse, to cramp its style—
Credit it, or not!
So, sidle up to it I do,
And raise my wrathful wrist,
As hate becomes its Waterloo
Beneath my crushing fist...
But, more than that, it didn't budge,
And, as it died, it shed
Blood viscous as the chocolate fudge
Still buried in my head.

SUNDAY TIMES

Eight

If Sunday times are often good,
Sometimes they may be black:
Sometimes we stack more firewood
Than winter's lack can hack...
And so, we up and go to church—
To keep the dogs at bay,
And knock the Devil off his perch,
Before he's gotta pray!
This tyrant, true, is of a view
(His wish is my command)
I carry Cinderella's shoe
In someone else's hand...
For who am I to emulate
That death-defying feat:
To whisk a woman, *tête-à-tête*,
As patriarch *élite*,
To where my choice is chalk or cheese,
In Sunday times we plumb
On dreary Mondays—sure to please
The glorious, and glum!

BRAGGADOCIO

Nine

If, lonely, just one wish, for thee,
Were mine to conjure up,
Thou only must, complicitly,
Survive a wee pre-nup—

As Bam-Bam, Dino, Pebbles yon
Libretto, lyrics, lines
You pen (depending on a wan
And dire critic's signs)

Combine the Stone Age with tomorrow's
Tuppence, for to fill
A quill you borrow, killing sorrow—
If a penny will

Captivity impose, a rose's
Petals turn to frost:
As quivers shiver guns, in prose's
Mettle stern, emboss'd!

CAPTAIN HOOK

Ten

Thou shalt not, shalt not, Moses, Friend,
What's writ commit to pieces:
You're better till the bitter end,
When, woken, *something* ceases...
To call the Lord a *stranger*—vinyl's
Rubbish, ain't it? Gas!
But you're no hero in the Finals:
Light squares mix'd with Mass...
"Deceiver of the Nations": Now,
Pray tell us whose to-do
Will fit our designations—bow
Wow, couldn't that be you?
To be, in spite of what you blurt,
No saviour to *rapport*,
'Tis taste through which our hearts get hurt—
A good-for-nothing's war,
Who, backwards tracking ev'ry book
That counts, 'neath *yellow* suns,
Goes Hell for leather—*Captain Hook*
Recording rhyme that runs!

SON(G)YA

Eleven

To eyes no *coup d'état* belongs
No *coup de fil* to ears:
If any to you say *"Maman"*,
So be as *Belle* appears!

May love, which fills this silly song,
Waltz happily, to be
A ripple on your billabong—
In dancing repartee

Insistence waking to the task
Of Moses, carting knaves
For Sister Sonya's inner flask
Of roses, parting waves

In Fields above Elysian—
To live, and never die,
Our song of songs Parisian
She's singing for the sky.

TO DEPART

Twelve

The autumn falls, the winter comes,
The spring may spring its reign—
But, here and now, the summer humbles
Hope, to wax and wane...
Nefarious dews, heather's parts
Together in demence
Precarious, lose weather charts
Whose follies fillies sense
Ensnaring us—crude leather'd hearts
Of fail'd, jail'd gents
Who rule our *kinder* sanctuary,
Feigning free to fly,
Like older brothers: Thank-you very
Much—I want to cry,
Since *you*, my Princess, wish to see
Not artfulness in all
Those plovers, herons, blissfully
Engaging—would enthral
Two hearts, to take a single shot
At being understood:
But, until then, forget me not,
And smile—*you* for good!

FISH FOR TEA

Thirteen

Good Lord—in this establishment
They dish up fish for tea!
But on a Sunday? Lavish bent—
Albeit I can see
'Tis (more or less) vernacular
That promises to be
Deplorably spectacular
For beings just like me!

They'd pass me rather, but palaver
Turns from bolts to nuts:
Cashews, pecans, ones from Java,
But demeaning struts
Into my gullet, like a bullet
Piercing through my guts—
Pull it, Man, the Little Lamb
I'm relishing to cheer,
Adds pearls to this carousing clam
You're nourishing, to jeer!

LOVE'S BALLET

fourteen

She shimmies on my bed, alone
She sees me prancing there—
Through moves so good we don't postpone
Her Shostakovich flair...

Where do you tarry, lover mine?
I slowly go insane—
To greet your cherry blossom, dining
On my flaccid brain!

Your beauty is for me, you know,
So, give it not to them—
Just charlatans trapp'd in their snow-
Bound streets you won't condemn...

And so, we sow the seeds of dreams
Together into one
Desire for the higher Star
Who steams the morning Sun.

SHE SENT ME KISSES

Fifteen

Between the two of us, she misses
Bona fide Heaven-sent
Connection—as she sent me kisses,
Tell me where forever went!

Egyptians, Greeks, the Romans, others
Never thought their time was up,
Until 'twas done—communion smothers
Hopes a fading buttercup

Ingests, to be with her: the Jewel,
Eden's ample water-tap—
His mistress of desire who'll
See him sample, sought, her sap!

SILVER LININGS

Sixteen

If I am thirteen, but a day,
I'm fifty-eight in years—
Oh, see the ocean cut away
Its pebbles into tears!

A glass for me is never empty,
Nor shall Truth contain
The Love-to-Be I'm ever gently
Thirsting to explain...

Shall I ascend, Queen Daffodil,
To sip your spirit's water?
Well, maybe not, so yet I still
Awake to take my daughter

Up in arms she's pining for—
Her incandescent cloud
A veil for silver linings, sure
To shine on Papa's shroud!

FRANKLY, MY DEAR ...

I do, in awe, reiterate
How best she is to see:
Shy wooing bore me wit—to mate
Erotic Italy,
So far beyond a notional
Persuasion I decree,
To love: *Amore*'s potion all
Must drink, including me!
I store no stash of other moves—
To heat up inner light's
Lugubrious, less soothing grooves,
In search of nicer nights:
I chase her freckles' dancing frown,
Lest, toss'd in derring-do,
I drown beneath her eiderdown,
My posture bury two
Poor orbs inside the dove I love—
That, should survival meet
Realities, she don a glove
For my *ti amo*, neat!

ANAROSA

Eighteen

Amen, a man for woman—
Goddess, God did good in thee:
For She has pipp'd me, like a lemon
Falling from His apple tree!

True lover mine, we must design
Erotic lines, devotionals to be
Sent south of Eden—even wine
Off *Yarra* vines deserves a piece of *Brie*!

The thorn they scorn this very morn,
Too late for *gai Paris*,
Re-born may, torn his merry lawn,
Woo Fate, or lay decree

To purge of turgid words a lurgy's
Guv lent Easter, re
The splurge of surging birds emerging
Luvvy-duvvily!

THE SKYLARK'S DANCE

Nineteen

There is a dance, there is a song,
Too beautiful to me—
We were together, all along,
In tune, in time, in thee.

The skybird lays his skylark's praise
Like honey onto toast—
Too thick to drizzle, sweet to graze
On, not to be her most

Fanatic champ: To light her lamp
Each moment with his touch,
His glowing knowing showing damp
Collusion with how much

In peace, in candour, Heaven's bloom,
In Frangipani's truth,
May be *pronto soccorso,* womb
In which we seal youth!

CHAMPIONNE DE L'UNIVERS

She loves her master, flowers too,
Me owing nothing more—
She loves my nature, music through
Our windows, to a door...
Her palace is a pleasure dome
She's living in—to tout,
Within this tome, the home I roam
In, pondering her pout—
Unable so to label stable
Features of my ploy,
As, glancing up, our kitchen table
Witnesses her joy:
For, high upon the fridge, so proud,
She's clever as the Sun
That re-appears, before a cloud
Can do what must be done...
"La Championne de l'Univers"—
A sniffer on the watch—
Almighty Aphrodite purrs
In songs mere mortals botch!

SPLEECH PINPRESS

Twenty-One

Forget all hist'ry, at thy peril
Win the hon to come—
Attacking outlaws, foxy, feral,
Dutifully dumb!

Let him be thy lad, my Lady,
Let his voice subdue—
Lest, in herst'ry, drive thee crazy
Mysteries, a new

Dimension—to thy succour
Fortunate, O Fuzz,
Call police, to earn thy tucker—
Triple Zero buzz

And I shall save thy priceless shell
From lacking others' care—
This spleech impledimental spell
To be-st'ry: White Knight's fare!

SOOT, SAND, STEAM, SALT

Twenty-Two

Our Star is nigh well gone for good,
Until she chooses pain
In someone else's neighbourhood,
To profit from a gain

Which, some contend, is but a loss—
A turning, trembling globe
Theatrical, with debts across
The *manna* of its probe,

Solicits Solomon, our Friend,
To set, and rise, and play
With hearts of humankind that end
Up helplessly as may

Be here below the skies, a cloud
Depositing raw soot—
In sand for steam a salt allow'd
To bury ev'ry foot!

THE BIG FELLA

Twenty-Three

Noti Ammo—good name for his band
You'd never hear him utter!
I stretch quadrangles in the sand:
Imagine him in butter!
Obscenities in high demand
From rockers self-adoring,
Who love their jobs, if second-hand,
When *Prozac*'s up for scoring...
He chooses prudently—snot pann'd
That Satan figures boring—
Compelling belles, he sells his spell
Too well, to tell how, smelling swell,
A fella's gotta go to Hell
To dwell through Papa's snoring!
He trends to mend, when, prior penn'd,
Book written from the end,
Lends limbs too trim for Jello gyms
To cymbals—on a nimble whim
His Etna's melting for him!

LOVE SONG

Twenty-four

Who is the one that loves me?
Mother, sister, song:
Her little heart ungloves me,
Neither risking wrong,
For, fecund as a dove, she
Settles to be strong
Below, before above we
Must, in time, belong...

Be still, my Darling, virtue's
Patience number one:
You'll see my calming gird you,
Seeing Time unspun
Requite my karma stirr'd, to
Sing our song in fun:
Attune gymkhana's words, glue
Ginger to the Sun!

FAR AWAY ON PAPER

Twenty-five

Your lover grieves for thee, his starling,
Far away on paper sings
A love song to, in comfort, Darling,
Court thy captive savourings.

How am I to re-quiet gentle
Loveliness *he* stole away?
I know a little sentimental
Loneliness be thine today:

If, in my heart, there lives a lavish
Overture, its piquancy
Permits a martyr head-long ravish
Clovers' purity—and thee!

ASH

Twenty-Six

Her locks will fox the oxen, Ash,
Our *fashionista* blonde—
Albeit less a vixen, passion
Tricks them to be fond!

This vixen's more adept, in flight,
T' accompany an eagle—
For ever since Lord Darwin's sight
Saw something in a beagle,

So many see no use for God:
Still, *she* will not concur—
I look into her mirror, nod
And see the God in *her*!

Perhaps she longs for me to hope—
To pick her up, and strip,
In serenades, each isotope
Of lippie off her lip!

WESTERN MAN

Twenty—Seven

Ironic 'tis to call him '*Guy*'—
My friend, the Western Man:
He isn't *veak*, far from it—why,
I do the best I can
To see him move, though not for me
His power plays, his quips,
Exposing what he's got for me:
Just lemonade he sips!

An idol, with his *Square Trade Chess*,
Might size up, cross the board,
Lest one go first, for, more or less,
Thus spake Caïssa, Lord—

"*Off with its head*!" he saith, in faith,
Of *kibitzers* in check:
For each of them is but a wraith
He's training hard to wreck!

MAMMA MIA!

Twenty-Eight

You bear your sash, your clever beau,
But now we part together—
Were I to search your Church, you know,
We'd fall asleep forever!

But you're still munching chalk and cheese
On Satan's three-day cruise—
To end up with a glass of lees,
In flip-flops mocking shoes!

You read minute *minutiae*,
You study bread, and whine
The way to nail *sushi*—I
Do not, a fish in brine!

You love your lamb, you love for good,
However, 'tis the end
Of boneless ham with lemon pudd—
My wholly holy Friend!

NIB SHARP & TARDY

Twenty-Nine

O Little Darling, heart of hearts,
A fox's dense sea dews
May draw, in pencil, keen deep arts—
Upon her mead 'n' mews

An aster, petals somehow fur:
She wants to play a harp—
For nipples hard to register,
And nib so tardy, sharp

As berries: Quicken lemon, lime,
Make wilt, as honey teems,
Her mats his candy caught in time—
Before tomorrow's dreams!

MARGARITA

Thirty

The air is fresh because of you—
Your being lights the dark:
You're Nature's ally in the Zoo,
For, loving as a lark,
Five keys a-cluster on your wrist
You clasp to keep me in
Your near vicinity, assist
My *quasi* bobby-pin!

Yes, thank-you, Wench, your accent is
As cheering as a chip
For seagulls, one of them a whiz
To you, his salmon dip!

However, Sister, take good care,
Beware, defer your grief—
For many men will drink you bare
T' ensnare your stirring leaf!

DESPOTS' DAME

Thirty-One

From the ceiling hangs a boxer—
Broken noses, in a frame—
Just a silly bobby-soxer
Born to lose? Oh, what a shame
Clueless kidults cannot fox a
Socialite who's worth the name!

Lilith's tongue for him is tempting—
Is she Russian, to be game?
Is she nineteen, is she twenty—
Maid to wither, whence she came?
God knows vanity's exempting
Lack of fortune, lack of fame,
From insanity pre-empting
Will she nips in buds, to claim...

Popping via Psyche's art, heart
Eros aims to set aflame—
Copping higher *Reiki*'s part, starts
Despots' Dame you'd betta tame!

DARK'S ARRIVAL

Thirty-Two

Two Kingdoms, two Monarchs
Will send out their Men
Empathic—if on Dark's
Arrival, to ken

When it's come, my Lady
(Our strongest of all)
Won't cry like your Baby
You bet will appal

Those lesser lights, regents
Who aren't worth their salt:
Whose *offence* is *defence*,
Not really their fault,

Since tactics and strategies
Please to preserve
And pickle their panoplies—
"*You've* got a nerve!"

WATERCRESS

Thirty-Three

I love your Pa (we love your Mamma, too)
Who, near-abouts this quintessential day,
Up-cream'd a beam in streaming dreams of *you*—
Who, tender true-purr, made this rascal stay!
Yea, bless us all below, let *Minne* be
Our plot to plunder picks 'n' pots 'n' pans—
I am your *Fischer's lovebird,* in a tree:
Octavian's cot free for all she fans...
For I do not enslave, nor do I fox
The one upon my heart, in time, in tune:
If I be counting chickens, Goldilocks,
(To dip inside your varicose lagoon)
Somehow you sing 'n' sell the times you tell—
Liszt, Mozart, eat your hearts out, make a wish—
To sup on ev'ry evening's inner gel:
Desire's twilight gamete, in a dish...
Wet, wondrous, woo'd, and worthy, welling lark,
Inside oncoming vestiges of light—
Your perfect match would burn up Noah's Ark,
To escort thoughts of watercress, tonight!

THE LEANING STARS

Thirty-four

I'm told in Heaven lean the stars,
Until they pause to think—
When they must stand like cable cars,
And fade from red to pink...

A beauty's in a bonfire—
Aghast, the Devil's dew,
A lute within a quagmire
His *"Sois Bienvenu!"*

For callous hit parades imply
The Winter isn't done
With mesmerizing, by and by,
The steaming morning Sun:

Nor flowing whither love won't show
(In lyricism bold)
And going slither, dove in toe—
A Saint, if truth be told!

ROCK'S GOLDEN TSAR

Thirty-five

Slug Satan, drag on, take a puff,
(I call a spade a spade)
Hug mates, and shag yon Pufnstuf—
Why, born to trade your shade,
You lie in bed, you liar, dead
I swear you'll never be—
For dying lead, to fire wed,
Might dare to, cleverly,
Embrace *the Book of Love* between
Its coming and its gone
Grim ace—*the Sook Above* unseen
Pits Dumbo and his wan
Assassin: Kill your brother, able
Man-in-Waiting—budge
(Alas!) until another sable
Canon's baiting sludge...
You'd be a lawyer, writer, Sir,
But you want *ev'ry*thing:
Lewd seer, buoy for bites—incur
Mutt's truant revelling!

MIRTH IN EARTH

Thirty-Six

The day *the Music* comes to town
Will be the day it dies
Avuncular—to have renown's
A prison, not a prize...

Your beautiful reward is gone—
Your wedding took the cake:
Let Adam do *da doo ron ron*
To crush *the Cobra*—snake!

In peace for us, tie heart to heart—
We'll put the rubbish out:
In times to finish, times can start
To see my lover doubt

A kiss upon unpainted lips,
A chance to labour charms—
When, after eating fission chips,
We'll dance to David's Psalms!

NICE PIE

Thirty—Seven

How long inside I think I know
This sanctuary thine:
And ever mine a rest from woe—
Men taking on a fine

And caring sweet retreat, we meet—
To heat and then defer
When, incomplete, thou ever neat
And sweet without demur,

To pocket inner honeycomb,
Art in my reach, so nigh—
To *seraphim* a funny tome
(Or two) be nice as pie.

HAPPY DAZE

Thirty-Eight

Oh, happy daze, now here in you!
A voice inside declares:
A shot of inner *Xanadu*
Has caught me unawares—

As, shining on, a lover sent,
We dwelt upon a page:
To be together's covenant,
Our chaperone the sage

Bright morning Star, so hot on me
His golden rays of youth—
Investing love's dichotomy
In thee, enduring truth.

ART ON MY HEART

Thirty-Nine

She is delight on night-time's mind—
Our Star is gone, in thought's *propos*—
Her art's upon my heart, inclined
To be what Love, autumnal, slow,
Yet sure, sweet, true, (the very kind
I never thought I'd ever know)
Lets grieve, go on their way, resign'd,
Its leaves, deciduous as woe...

I kiss tomorrow's dawning, see
Those hauntings flee, of days before—
Lest I be lost in love, in thee
I do (a skylark seeing soar
Beside the skybird's panoply
Of heart still beating, feathers' core)

Entrust to life the light within
Two birds in flight, O peregrine!

OOPS, MADE A MISTAKE!

forty

From Adam's marrow, on the morrow,
Came a maiden fair—
To keep a *novice*, free from sorrow,
Cast into despair!
Albeit over, bees in clover,
Bliss (in truth) too sheer:
The Asp created advocated,
Into Evie's ear,
A plan most pleasing to the palate,
Or, at least, to *hers*—
To eat his apple, Adam's mallet
Knowing pristine furs...
So, who's to blame? A royal game
Of novelties (or luck)
Makes hard to frame a picture lame
For ne'er the twain to buck!
Wow, anyhow, 'tis over now,
The Lord's Song came to nought—
Though some endow a Golden Cow
With power, milking thought!

HOTTIE

Forty-One

Adore you, Baby—what a God
Created such a scene:
Just picture you—too hot a bod
On Heaven's darling Queen!

Yeah, charts you climb—in parts sublime,
You sing, and dance, and pivot
Hearts inclined to Spartan rhyme—
In honey's tones exhibit

Angels' loves we pin above—Gal,
You leave Man on heat:
Desire's port and principal
You're snatching from defeat!

THE WHITE QUEEN

Forty-Two

Too beauteous to be the sky's
Allowance—dance in flight
Yon lovely lark, to lift in prize
Less luminary light,
O'er hillocks heavy with her cries:
Rest easily tonight...

She is, on snow, my sole toboggan—
Wonder on two wings—
In dreams I see my lambent log on
Firebirds she sings:
Too tremulous to be her Fogg's

Wan Phileas, in lanes
Erotic—lark enticing doggone
Teeming summer rains!

MONDAY'S LIGHT

Forty-Three

He loves her: body, heart, and soul—
Not least, the way she glistens
Dew, from Eden's grassy knoll...
Her beat, to which he listens!

So, Loverboy has got a girl—
He's knocking on her door—
He waves and whispers to a pearl
On starlight's misty shore,

That, somewhere on a Sunday's night,
Too late to wait on Fate,
Self-immolating Monday's light,
May love become her mate!

FOR MOTHER A ROSE

forty-four

I can't take you anywhere! Thanks
For sharing that with me!
If Jesus for Maria ranks
So highly, won't she see

That even now, two thousand years
(Like sentinels to snow
Descending on her cheeks in tears
She hopes will never go)

May carry her on high, in choirs'
Notes to be a nun's
Small mercies for those caught in fires,
And the *other* ones

Much lovelier: James, Peter, Paul,
Including her, as must
Exemplars, to be there at all,
She prays for—ever just.

ANATAYLIA

forty-five

'Tis not as though I see through eyes:
You're ev'rywhere within—
I long to clasp you with my thighs,
To keep the summer in!

Your body is ambiguous
To ev'ryone but me—
Allusions are ridiculous,
In thinking that of thee...

And in that distant palace home
I see you sink in fur,
As, in a wistful palindrome,
You hear my level purr.

INNOCENT
the
BUDS

∞ ∞ ∞

Sunlight's Dream *for Garf*

God help me, Love—and then you stir
Two felons into Paradise:
No other found to fluff your fur,
For, right beside you, in a trice,
I'm truly yours, lest, as it were,
Those brothers, merely mental mice,
In parting seas, O Puss-on-Purr,
(To make what isn't gentle nice)
Prefer blur's *imprimatur*—her—
To grace their table's lentils, rice,
Or gold, and frankincense, and myrrh,
From sugar's condimental spice!

She loves to live, and lives to love
Just me, my sweet *Paloma*—dove!

GRAVID WOOD

One

An ally, *a priori* wise,
Is whispering inside
A tom's dogmatic alibis—
Elision to elide
With *a posteriori* pinks,
On paperweights-in-two:
You'll end up inner noble, Minx,
All tangled up in blue!
Devotionals to skies imply,
That, winning her for good,
Dear Brahms, within his lullaby,
Will milk her gravid wood:
Apotheotic precedents
Combobulating pain,
To free of all impediments
Poseidon's purple chain
Around my neck—an *objet d'art*
Subsisting, in her wake:
The *Queen of Hearts* best trumping Mamma's
Cluey, clammy cake!

TEMPTATION'S THOMAS

Two

His she-cat's happy! Having eaten
To her heart's content,
He treats her to a *Chocolate Wheaten*'s
Trap *Nirvana* lent—
For he, Temptation's Thomas, tempting
Foolery she downs
In love for life's *bête noire,* exempting
Fudge to foil frowns,
Knows toms *are* toms, but *she*, so chic at
Purring, cannot find
A better one: Albeit weak at
Mastering his mind,
He lives in hope, for love to live,
And, living, never die,
For duty his 'tis e'er to give
Up pieces of his pie
To whiskers teaming bristle's dream
With elocution's punk—
As salmon, swimming up a stream,
Sac back, to go kerplunk!

INNOCENT *the BUDS*

Three

Autumnal comes the cherry blossom,
Somewhat out of whack—
Whoever owns this orchard, toss 'im
And 'is 'orrors back!
But no, 'tis but a dream, I doze
Night's God-forsaken mare—
I offer her, in peace, a rose,
And ride on, *debonair...*
For all about me, *épée* at
The ready to defend
My *Fleur de Lys*, my darling cat,
Or whomsoe'er I lend
Her honour's inner innocence—
The Reaper closing in
To skewer in a pin immense,
A dagger to my chin,
Delicious wishes for my Queen
With internecine studs:
As, throwing light on darkness seen,
Bloom innocent the buds.

A *VERY* GOOD PLAN!

four

We're marching into battle—we
Can take what's coming on:
I hear *purrfection* (that'll be
The harp you're strumming on)
As, 'midst the rubble, on the double,
Plummets into love
Designer stubble's *Kabul trouble*,
Settling like a dove,
To see me seek your face, your eyes
Unflickering, so held
To render wise, in hope's disguise,
A spruce, in time, be fell'd—
Allowing Faith to come to power,
Reckoning God's bud
So great as Solomon in flower,
Chewing on His cud...
What shall I do? I have a plan:
To love you till the end
Of time, before above began
Clap-trappiness on trend!

HONEY'S WONDER

five

A *Maserati* doesn't purr
So lovingly, nor mine
Shall bear a *Lamborghini*'s fur,
Ferrari on a vine
Of felt—to sip a vintage rare,
I hold her up in arms,
To sense heat radiate from where
Heart beauteous becalms...
What made communion smart that day,
Eleven years ago?
I feel zeal's dart that may
Let honey's wonder flow
To see her still: She's keeping me
So happy to re-live
The loving hours leaping we
(With nothing to forgive)
So consecrate, to never lose
Her clause to pause again—
Lest torque implore whatever choose
The flaws of poorer men!

'TIS *SHE* WHO LOVES

Six

Sometimes I don't turn on the lights—
Well, sometimes, *they* don't *me*:
What *Minne* singers, olden Knights,
Are searching for in thee,
Are sparklers borne crepuscular,
Like starlight through the mists
Of Time: If brawn, so muscular,
Tries opening its fists
Too slick for nickels, swallow dimes,
For clovers coalesce
In sonnetry—*not* hollow rhymes
Unable to compress
This lapping of a sigh within
That emptiness without
The Apple of the Eye we pin
Our teardrops to, in drought...
To understand, 'tis *she* who loves,
The One, before the rest,
Whose jaws align with foxy gloves
Too good—to better best!

ROYAL CROYDON

Seven

Let Arthur Boyd tread *Royal Croydon*,
Whispering your name,
As parts alloy'd, read in a void,
Eliciting more fame,
See, overjoy'd, a winner's buoy'd
To mate him, just the same!
In shades of Black your Men attack,
(To lack no knack of phrase)
Go *rat-tat-tat*, lest rampant sac
Your Grace in power plays
So *de rigueur*—for *szeretlek*,
Your *force majeure* conveys...
Agamemnon, *crème* upon
Your gladiator's sword
Is, but for scones a trifle wan,
(To cook your book's *fjord*)
Vicissitudes of dark and light,
Once playing on a brow:
What then was passion, now is trite
Concession, we allow!

VIGNETTE

Eight

The whole world says it loves you—
If loving understood
The lengths Desire's Dove flew,
To settle, as it should,
On friends and family fortunate,
As beauteous and blest—
Allow me, so importunate,
Exonerating jest,
Request alliance secretly
Be somehow here on stage,
Where many lie less piquantly
Impaled on a page:
To say how greatly I admire
Friendship I adore
With Loveliness from Heaven's choir,
On a distant shore—
Which, Empress, given art in thee,
Empathic ev'ry gram,
Inspires love, impartially,
To spread your bread with jam!

AZALEA

Nine

'Twas in the beginning
True love was created,
Before spaces spinning,
And species related,
Saw God no more winning
Than Knights Errant mated!

But high on a rocky ledge
Buds an Azalea—
Up for the privilege
Of Anataylia,
Hedging to gently fledge
Songs of Australia...

To leave her, I love her—
Her beauty won't fade,
If Heaven's above her:
Elysian Maid!

QUEEN'S PAWN

Ten

'Midst all doom and gloom, pray pontificate whom
I'm sure to adore, winsome, wanton, and white,
When witches converge, less than lovingly loom
To thwart her accession, French-kissing the night...
Should I die a warlock, wolf-whistle, or wait,
In wishing her wardrobe impermanent clad,
Just leading her on, until stale the mate—
To tabulate lessons on *abaci* mad?
No, Earth is her ambit—she smelters the Sun,
Drags Moons from their orbits, sees Stars, in their way,
Let *pathos* undo what is yet to be done
To love lost at twenty-one, praying for prey...
Too right, *clean the White Queen*, still ruling the board,
Is Heaven I'm harbouring: Send me to Hell,
If *ma ma ma Belle* isn't loving the sward
Of dew made for savouring—gem's jolly gel!

SOMEWHERE MY ELEVEN

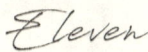

Somewhere my Eleven is gasping for air—
My Forty-Two, Sixteen, my bright Fifty-One—
He'll bottle her, label her, wrap her with care,
And swear that he's innocent: Knight shift begun!
For fire, in sweeping through blankets of wool,
(Thank God *she*'s no Little Lamb, leave that to *me*!)
Conspires to rescue her, stamp like a bull
The embers beneath her, incongruously!
If *I* had my way, just a little bit odd,
I'd see her inside of me, taking him on,
Instead of which *she*'s keeping Faith *à la mode*—
His ever to be one to never be gone!
I'd steal her fitfully, if but I could
Make hope more gratuitous, dignity's sum
Maid Marian precious, whom I, Robin Hood,
In keeping her intimate, under my thumb,
Would hold to my heart, inner forest of trees
Supposedly *Sherbrook*, a watery drain
Becoming a locket, a home to a breeze,
To fill us till spirit's will's trusty—and sane!

COMPANION PEACE

Twelve

If knowing thee, we find it, Friend,
The Love my Faith mistook,
Our poetry's behind it—penn'd
Above, in space, this book!

A miracle's peach crouches on
The doona on my bed—
As, lyrical, each doubter's gone,
For, tuning yonder thread,

Here, 'twixt my chalice and some woods,
'Twas serendipity's
Cheer fix'd thy palace, handsome goods,
'Cos (mention'd wittily)

You *are*, possess'd, love letter's best
Cat-beast (bless me, I shock!):
New Darma's guest, doves let, carress'd,
Pat ceaselessly, *ad hoc*!

TUNA BAKE

Thirteen

I love thee, Tuna Bake, as though
I were to love myself—
A kookie Cupid, heart aglow
On pyre's upper shelf—
O soul, horizon's horror far,
Art borne a bulbous moon,
Thy spirit's inner pickle jar
Bereft of hope and spoon
To scallop thee: *God, let me drown,*
Or, trapp'd in here, I swear
He'll pine to pin your purple gown—
Semblable, mon confrère...
Who bringeth light, on him I call,
Yes, Lucifer, the same:
To Earth he fell, as angels fall,
As luminous he came—
With whom I share this love of life's
Creation, good as God's
Enfants terribles, caught in strife's
Panache, against the odds!

JUDGE MENTAL

fourteen

Judge not, lest thou be judg'd, 'tis said,
Though, mentally a rogue,
He cut his lip, till judgment bled,
So brutally in droplets fed
More sentences in vogue...

O Brother, you are such and such!
O Mother, harlot thou!
O Lover, let me touch as much
As, propp'd upon a cranky crutch,
Behoves a holy cow!

Howbeit, if he call me *this*,
&/or he call me *that*—
However hard he hone his hiss—
I'd answer: *'Tisn't mine to kiss*
Dear John, Mark, Luke, or Matt!

SPRING EQUINOX

Fifteen

When the light in her eyes
Sees the days inner lift,
And the bowerbird cries,
My polarities shift—

And the love in my heart
For the woman in her
I should readily thwart,
If I could, to defer

The conclusions of night
In the blessings of morn—
As her petals, affright,
Ponder roses in thorn.

SUNNY

Sixteen

Your love's in the sky, and
I'll write you a song:
A *dactyl*, an *iamb*,
To right ev'ry wrong—
It's raining where *I* am,
Not where *you* belong!

Our Sunny's inside us,
You're here in my heart;
Lest hope be denied us,
The Sun cease to chart
On weather maps—hide us
In clouds drawn apart...

So, thank-you for shining,
For, never to end,
More stars are aligning
Than one may depend
On—never resigning:
True friend for a friend!

BIRDS & BUMBLING BEES

Seventeen

So, this all came from nothing—
Redheads lit the match?
If animate's the cussing
Driven to dispatch
The wattles and the clovers,
Birds and bumbling bees—
Will kisses between lovers,
Conquering the breeze,
Arrive at Hope's conclusion?
Cold *tsunami* seas
Enlisting shore's collusion,
Craving to appease!
The very one I worship,
One I must adore,
I liken unto rosehip
Press'd into a pore,
Which, blossoming to answer
Dew upon my skin,
In bright sparks of a dancer
Champions my chin!

CHANSON D'AMOUR

Eighteen

Your *song of love* is on the air—
I wrote it just for you:
Our clefs and trebles dazzle where
My words, of azure hue,

Make melodies ecstatic float
On particles of light—
To synchronize your woollen coat,
Cute boots, and frilly white

Frisson, a blouse you smile, style
Sure to thaw my pen:
Albeit poor in spirit—trials'
Happiest of men!

PARIAH

Nineteen

No friend is she—I am alone,
She works for me, no more:
This bleak pariah, set in stone
My heart, cut to the core,

Is empty—broken is the man,
Her vivisection's toll;
On fire in a frying pan
My shatter'd, shameful soul

Without redress—no ling'ring hopes
To settle spirit's dove
Abandon'd, on the slipp'ry slopes
Of disappearing love.

SUNSHOWER

Twenty

No word as yet—a single sign
To stop the rain, to make
This heart of periwinkle thine,
Adrift on Lover's Lake...

Still, I must keep the thought of thee
Inside, to bottle, warm,
Those pools which, aching, court the sea
Outside, beneath the storm—

As, of a sudden, shining through
The droplets which descend,
I see the sun defining you:
True evermore my friend.

NOT THE ONE

Twenty–One

Collecting stamps, my lover lately
Is a memory—
Philately must end, a stately
Stratagem, or three,
Impenetrable: Woman, thou
Art lying on a lawn,
Recumbent on a green—how now,
Forgotten delta's dawn...
Whatever's done, I'm *not* the one,
So penn'd, to recommend
A git: *To whit*, who's got my thunder—
Stole it, to defend
This ink he's linking, artful, old,
To *ova* bred to wed
Display he's made of, you remould
From gold, to pink, and red...
For wines, too ripe on summer vines,
Too hesitant for crops,
Are vinegar for dumber lines—
Whose presence winter cops!

BEAUTY SPOT

Twenty-Two

Contented in the Sun she lies,
Directing, from her chair,
The world with omnipresent eyes—
His Little Girl so fair:

In essence ev'ry bit of thee,
Within a beauty spot,
His artistry's epitome,
Divine forget-me-not,

Which, to encapsulate in ink,
Creation doth elude—
Except for Him, whose love in pink,
Miraculous construed,

Combining nose's inner edge
With ginger gentle, soft,
Is one Creator's privilege
For fashioning, aloft.

SORROW IN CONCEPTION

Twenty-Three

The genesis of sorcery—
'Tis crying from the ground:
Thy mother knew debauchery
In thee, to make a sound
Of sorrow in conception, so
Begat thee into strife,
As, tempted by deception, woe
Took weakness for a wife...
"Am I my brother's keeper?" Well,
Just possibly—to Nod
Thou shalt be cast, as if to Hell
A godly staff and rod
Once pure, winning Satan's bin
Original and old:
Hans Wooer pinning Pater in
His excremental gold...
For lovers settle in a heart
Of sacramental wine,
But, God knows, thou must soon depart
For Hades—less benign!

WOULD I STILL LOVE

Twenty-four

Would I still love, demure, sweet,
Purrfection's slumb'ring Queen,
Whose jaws on paws in purring meet
Fragility serene

On loving lap—wert thou not mine
To gaze upon, in awe,
And deem eternal beauty thine
My quest forevermore?

Lest from this moment, growing old,
In heart I grow not numb,
A wish to catch thy marigold
Within my frail sum

Will take thy joyous ginger eyes
Up into outer space
With me—that lovers not despise
The tears upon my face.

STOLEN STARSHIPS

Twenty—five

Well, hello Gorgeous, clever Cookie,
Papa's little Angel Possum
Fortune found, ere Heaven took thee
Back to God, so strange a Boss—whim

Evermore my friend, betwixt
Love beauteous, in fur a-purr,
And confluence of Fates, affix'd
In Stolen Starships, as it were...

My rigmarole's got what her soul's
Cajoling—as aromas waft,
I bid my *rôle*'s lot not too droll:
Extoling my *Paloma* soft!

PERFECT TWELVE

Twenty-Six

Thou shalt not covet—whisper that
As I survey his wife:
The Weather Goddess, belly fat
And full of foreign life
For him and his sophisticate—
Oh, cut me with his knife!

My *perfect twelve*—much more than *ten*—
Art *Woman*, and they know it:
Lord Byron, and the other men,
Who'd sacrifice, to show it,
Their soon, their now, their origin—
To see your all below it!

THE LIFE IN A LEAF

Twenty—Seven

Where does the life in a leaf go,
When the leaf leaves?

Whence comes the life in a leaf, Love,
When the spring springs?

And whither the wall of silence
In the leaf,
When the autumn falls?

Where does the life in a leaf go,
When the leaf leaves?

Post Script:

A
SHOT
of
LIGHT

∞ ∞ ∞

The **Question** *for Her*

'Nirvana Love'

Lest I seduce thee via song,
A western Hall of Fame
Is where I found my heart belong—
For yours, of gold, my claim...

God, 'twasn't I to bold enquire
How your kindly Ma,
Or bountiful your proud *Esquire*,
Shibboleth and *Shah*,

Upon a name so clearly true
Did happen: but 'twas thou,
With sunlight sparkling, inner dew,
Who ask'd of me, somehow...

And two years later I have laid
My roving eyes aside:
O dear *Claudine*, if someone pray'd
For someone else, they lied!

Lover of My Cells

The 'Opening'

Delight and Darkness, she and he
Togetherness apart
From all Creation yet-to-be
Omnipotent, by heart...
Link up this lonely hand in yours—
Before the skies attend
This miracle of you, on shores
To break, but never end
Those waves of peace, yon lovely lash
A wet and wild flood
To be this *passionisto*'s pash
Your hyacinth in bud,
Or silver fern, in nights to come,
O Lover of My Cells:
In whom I hope, sweet juicy plum,
This prune I am indwells
A woman young and wondrous, mine
To pamper and protect,
If, giving *Pellegrino* thine,
Love bubbles intellect!

Long Time, No See

The 'Middle Game'

Her happy heart, a *palanquin*
To answer ev'ry quest
I'm landing on—a gal akin
To loveliness compress'd,
Asleep on very vestiges
Of green and gold velour
Wrapp'd in her—too blest, I guess,
This night's erotic tour
To rouse *the Universal Queen*
To wait upon this day,
When Hell's been done, by Heaven seen,
Divining what's to say
Of servants, snakes, and sycophants,
Too quick to swallow pills,
To kill or quell what militance
Requires of their ills...
Oui, c'est la vie—unless it's not,
When death, or something worse
Will soon erase that apricot
They smile, like a curse!

Midnight

The 'End Game'

I wish, for thee, tomorrow come,
To make of darkness light:
Queen Guinevere, adhere Tom Thumb
(Arthurian and white)
To clocks left ticking on a ledge
You never knew before;
To wet a moat around a hedge,
So feminal and raw,
Is *my* responsibility—
I ask of Heaven's gong,
And that with due civility,
If writing makes me wrong,
To ponder thee each time I ope
My heart to see inside
Our fairy tale, hoping Hope
And Fortune will collide—
Or whether bleeding, pleading art,
As stealthy as a stone,
Will disconnect your weather chart—
Convulsing to condone!

How Long Have I Known Thee

The 'Post Mortem'

I seem to recognize you, in
The Woman of my Hopes
An epoch earlier—to win
The One, with whom elopes

A *sick* and saucy vagabond
You concentrate, to serve,
As I resign my magic wand,
To cover ev'ry curve

That concentrates, in turn, *forsooth*,
Each paean meant for *you*,
By relics worthy of your youth
And beauty—tried and true...

So, how long have I known thee, Lynx,
O Lover of My Cells?
Black Caviar is courting Winx,
If Kingston Town rebels!

Post Post Script:

'DOKTOR VILE'
&
'DAME LADY JANE'
&
'SUZANNAH'

∞ ∞ ∞

'DOKTOR VILE'
[*for* **Cumquat-May**]

Take a seat—yes, *any*where,
(To which we'll have to point)—
We know it isn't justice fair,
But papers us anoint!

> Who *am* I, Docs—pleas can't Ewes 'ear?
> Per'aps, Watt's betta left
> To Rudolf, lest Rose-Aysha clear—
> And *Ewes* (of cares bereft)
> Will tell me times, for Keys in clocks,
> Like Bridges on a stage
> In Freo—day make woks dat shocks
> For Tuna's inner Cage!

But tell us—don't you miss your cat??

> Well, not until Ewes cited
> The One I Love, to give a pat—
> Percase I'm still invited!

What bought you here, we'd like to know?
Is someone 'id inside
To make you pack up bags, to shew

How cucumbers (if fried)

Can't help but—hang on, wait a mo'—

It isn't *you* we chide

For faking *catatonia* (though

Sigmund never lied)—

If only Edgar Allan Poe, so

Living, till he died

Of poetry and sorrow, *Dodo*'s

Witness, country-wide,

Could be this day's diurnal rose,

Delivering *the Guide*

To base your base-line's *con*'s and *pro*'s

On, simpering and snide...

But *Sugar Candy Mountain*'s woes

Will wipe out what we sigh'd,

To chisel on your tombstone—*Ho*

Ho Ho, at least he tried!

Yeah, yeah, I tried, orright, allow

The Boss to count acclaim,

To whom must answer even *thou*—

Down Underneath, aflame!

Ewes peek-a-boo, if worth a plough

The Earth inside my lame

Seclusion here, 'midst swine and sow,

As *kosher* as *The Game*

For *lunatoid arthritics*: *Tao*

For Jill, and Jak, and Jame
A catalyst, as *Chairman Mao*
(Or *Dan*—they're all the same!)
Must realize I prize my *Frau*—
Well, *bitte schön*, Ewes tame
Me with *Temazepam*'s kapow,
In *Schadenfreude*'s name...
So, let us tell Ewes, 'ear 'n' 'ow
Nobody suffers pains—
Exceptions being peers 'n' chows
Ewes drizzle down our drains!!

[So, save us, Jesus, come in clouds—
The Way Ewe went before
Styx prickle sickles into shrouds
Of loveliness ... and WAR!!!]

'DAME LADY JANE'

No housewife—to our merry house
Thou be not wed, on cred, nor marr'd—
To play piano's sherry nous,
Ne'er *en retard* we karmic sparr'd,
Before the Sun—*compadre* scarr'd—
Could be a spade of ways to prey
On grey, lest stay in plays of lard—
So problematically hard,
This day:
Our *Queen of Hearts*, in cakes you bake
For neighbours (give the milkman one!)
Was neither your intent a garden rake,
Nor *cherubim* for Cherry's finger-bun...
No: Synoptically, what you make,
Of what I spake, in song's mistake—
For love of raspb'ry's wan namesake:

Dear Mamma, I raid lemonade,
From nests, an egg or three, Mermaid,
I now—with feathers splay'd, outlaid—

Purr-suède—in palisades, for thee!

'SUZANNAH'

Suzannah speaks of peace, in roses
Trellises set free—
Hosanna's shrieks unleashing Moses
Walking through her sea!

His fleeting prim and proper princess
(Given unto Hope)
Is seeking love, where love is sinless
Heaven on a rope

She's wishing me—perhaps her smitten
Death-defying rod:
The One-to-Be, with whom a bitten
Breath-belying bod

Should fly up on an eyrie's ledge—
Bald eagle, one so high,
Born once upon a time, to wedge
Tuition to the sky...

Yet, I am I—perhaps a say in
Who may yet be whose,
Am putting off a pen to play in
Choosing to bemuse:

Serene, come autumn, bed down drops
In clusters on her path
So green—some orange, red-brown crops,
In gusts or fronds her bath

To bathe in we believe in—ours
The eagle and the hawk:
A skylark for the skybird's showers,
Squeaking into squawk

A sonnet's dreams for streaming cream—
Sue plans in ladles lost
Along wit's teeming seams I deem
Suzannah's cradles cross'd...

Yep, love is love that came and went,
Before it was at all:
Mix broken seconds with cement—
At beck and bloody call!

FRAGMENTS
(All for Thee)

∞ ∞ ∞

Jamie Shaw

"Well may Love be the Answer,
For 'tis clearly the Question..."

'From Time's Beginning'

From time's beginning thee I have adored,
And from thy soul's inception I thee knew;
In love for thee shall be my soul's reward,
And radiant e'er shall be my being's hue:

Thou shalt me comfort in life's cold duress,
And be for life's disease sufficient balm;
And thou—in turn—shalt care for my caress,
Each interloper shall I swift disarm—

That thou should'st know: thou art my love supreme—
The One I ne'er shall squander, nor regret;
The One in whom I trust, of whom I dream,
The One, in hope, I, countenancing, met...

Yea, thou shalt ever in a heart reside,
True, truant lover, loving cannot hide.

'Garf'

A field of butterlilies,
Tender style—
She will ever be, an effervescent sea,
Her soul on smile.

The loveliest of all
The roses,
Hopes adorning her:
Amidst the thorns,
She scampers on my lawns—
To best redoubters, cuts her shutters,
In bliss, at jellied prawns!

> (She isn't who I thought she was—
> So much more than a cat—
> Biography so short, becos
> I'm leaving it at that!)

'Bobby'

If left to write there was one pristine page,
Our God, in love, would leave it just for you:
The greatest of them all, in tender age
Confounding Muscovites, once well-to-do.

They say *the Art of Chess* is loath to press
True greatness into Man, yet I must think
(To quote, in eloquence, one proverb less)
You here supply the journey, I the ink...

You read encyclopaedias, and yet
Humility's the train of thought you catch:
If ever you alight, the Stars will set—
And sacrifice, to love, your perfect match!

'Guy'

A big fish in a little pond?
Recant your blasphemy!
You'd posit one of willing wand,
To curb his majesty:

But contradict the hypocrite,
Then annotate the Lie,
To blitz men in the grip of it—
Or, failing that, to try:

And he will spill his wit in words,
Like flowers at your feet—
Ranunculi for pretty birds,
Potatoes for their meat...

For he is like a fisher, not
The one to fall for bait:
Each brilliant *coup*, each crushing *shot*,
Is *force majeure*—Checkmate!

'Song for Jane'

You say, you have to go;
I say, why don't you stay:
You say, I'll never know
To pray for yesterday...
Darling, in my arms
You feel soft and warm,
But when you go, alarms,
And quakes, and qualms, and storms,
Take hold of me, and don't
Release me, till I find
That, loving you, I won't
Let loving from my mind...
For shadows on my mind
All cede, to be with you,
So sweet, and true, and kind—
A love alive and new,
Who knows just how to be,
Just how to look and love:
Who makes the man in me
An eagle for your dove!

Snatches

Let's generate love—
Wherever we meet,
A simmering stove
Of simmering heat!

Tu es, quand même, en cœur
Une fleur, mon amie fraîche:
Une vraie, bonne crème de sœur
Sans peur, qu'on, aimant, lèche!

Tu es la chanson bonne,
Le poème de mon âme;
Une chatte dedans ronronne
La vie, que tu entames!

The Goddess of my Heart,
She brews the Love I send:
Book written from the Start—
And starting at the End.

'Snags, Snubs, Snatches, Snitches, Snippets, Sniggers, & Snarls'

∞∞∞

'Quaint, Quizzical Quatrains'
—From the Quill of—
Jamie Shaw

Toulouse, or not Toulouse—
There sitting, all alone,
Marie: amidst the yews,
To adoration prone †

Let *love* be long, let *she* be mine
Whom, all along, my sole design
Made parallel—
To intertwine †

To find a move the engines can't
Is witchcraft, more than Chess:
Just like the seed, before the plant,
Was *D'Urberville* as *Tess* †

Living, breathing beauty thine
I bottle in my heart—
In love with ev'ry leonine
Purrfection you impart †

If Woman is perfection,
None created until her,
My natural selection
Is a pussy—*born to purr* †

Innocence is what I see
In thee, my *Turtle Dove,*
As, high above hypocrisy,
You soar, shy *Myrtle Love* †

Halfway through December, I
Can feel, on my lap,
The one I do remember, by
Surreal songs we trap †

Twelve years ago, *the Ides of March,*
Did boom a happy song—
Thee finding, where did overarch,
In zeal, thy sarong †

I cannot let you go, you see,
Unwritten by my pen—
Whose sole intent, to capture thee,
Is now: *Pray, tell me when* †

Yet, rest a while, *Little One,*
& I shall crown thy brow
With distant kisses, writ in fun—
In *pawtraiture*'s meow †

Lo, she doth just a kitten sleep,
No trouble sought, nor sown:
Subsumed by her subconscious deep—
So verily unknown †

If bats are in my belfry, now
Depicting thee *adorbs,*
Meows mistake a selfie—how
This camera bedaubs †

Binnen ein paar Nächten
Kommt der Weihnachtsmann:
Bester aller echten
Lügner—dann und wann †

Joyeux Noël à toi, ma Chère:
Laquelle, qui sais bénir
Les gouttes, qui, dans ma sèche bière,
Remplissent ton revenir †

OMG, *the Anti-Hero*
Of inclement scenes,
Knows how to move, in clouds he clears—
Ghost to pubescent teens †

Whither, *Frangipani,* gone
Be thou, my sweet lament?
My heart is seeking thee—a swan,
As thine, link'd erstwhile, rent †

So, I'm a brute—a trifle cute,
Till men in little coats
Of white *no player can refute*
Condemn my brittle quotes †

The telly blazes present crazes—
Do I hear my name?
The Moon, *God knows,* in crescent phases,
Smiles, just the same †

I ate a Christmas cookie, *tit*
For tat this cat's design—
No fish, no lamb, no chook, see fit
To laud, on which to dine †

Sweet can never parting be,
If you I can't forget
Through days of gentle revelry,
Delicious in regret ✝

We saw today, as butterflies,
How time from you doth flee,
The more you may cuss utter lies—
Now *Truth shall set you free* ✝

Say, *wherefore art thou,* asking *why*—
Far better question than
Just wanting, of a roamin' guy,
To *GPS* the man ✝

Yet, you will truly *shuffle off*
This mortal coil, when
This turning, trembling globe would doff
Its hat, to foil men †

'Tis early morn, so Our Star
Doth not requite, above,
Hearts beating *Heaven's Eye*—so far
Beyond inscription's love †

But thirty-seven plays, *my Lord*—
Yep, *all the World's a stage*
Phenomenal: Across the board,
He'd size you up, per page †

Shall I compare thee duly to
A Dobermanic Pincer?
So loyal she, & thou, whose truly
Mincing words evince her †

Tell: *Are you married yet?* saith he,
Unto desire's pet;
Well, maybe not, so marry *me*—
Won beauty Maya's debt †

Who is it, *sore Madonna,* we
See creeping, whither went
Due visits—for a wannabe
Ye, leaping, thither sent? †

Whatever floats our boats are rote's
Admissions, in the main—
As bread & butter's anecdotes,
In search of *Charlemagne* †

"Ein Sprachgenie"? Verzeihe mir
Mein Unvermögen doch,
Wenn jemand schreit: "Au weihe!", dir
Zerpreisend, was verkroch †

La Belle Époque de l'Homme venue,
La dolce vita qua:
L'on est content, déja vécu—
Quo vadis, vado, va †

I don't have a number, Son—
He's telling us the score:
Four hundred nil!—my #1,
Dost equalize the Law †

Lest hearts, in grief, two eyes deceive,
Gens Una Sumus, we
Must, rustily, just then believe—
If incredulously †

We Are One People, born to lie
Unsinkably as whales;
So, many of us live—to die
Unthinkably as nails †

Riches, all the rage, right now,
For *Lucy in the sky*—
Believing love contagious, wows
Kids, eating humble pie †

For what may profit (someone said)
The Kingdoms of the Earth
To gain—to find there burièd
Thy soul, devoid of worth? †

A man, two thousand years afar,
& almost human—true—
Departed Earth a *Superstar:*
As rose infecting dew †

Hyperbole is like a ball
Of sunshine in the rain—
Mere men who make the team recall
Their steam for *Lois Lane* †

More popular than Jesus is
One sister, born to be
(By hook or crook) forever His
Ineffability †

So, will she choose the football teams,
To source tomorrow's hunk?
I thought I heard her put all dreams
To bed—to peddle spunk †

Yet, what is time, if not with her?
The purring of a heart
Forsworn to love *Excalibur,*
As sharp as Eden's dart ✝

What's on my mind is so inclined
To whisper love I seize—
From thine so fine I find design'd
By pyrotechnic squeeze ✝

Love is when you add an 'R'
Unto devotion's pens—
The engine of a *Jaguar*
To purr, what never ends ✝

Grace is when you, undeserving,
Rise above the crowds
Belligerent, unnerving—prizing
Cotton-woollen clouds †

Parting sweet can never be
From her, on whom I bet
Whole-heartedly, yet cleverly
Delicious in regret †

If thou, *my Cheetah,* quick & cool,
Yet photogenic be,
I'd profit from *the Golden Rule—*
& make *the Artist* me †

At whose behest a Bishop best
See crazily *the Foe*
Contest arrest—a wish, obsess'd,
We lazily bestow †

O Queen, behold thine *errant Knight*—
I'm thinking he, thy friend,
Must apprehend a cosmic Light,
Which he would e'er defend †

Bull at a gate, beweeping loss,
Apart from Eden's dew—
The Prince of Darkness, born to cross
Forever's clever glue †

Sympathies! On fire, boys,
You had to hold your pens—
Not quite the gig for choirboys
On any trips or bends †

Settle, Petal, show your mettle,
Lest, in Satan's dew,
You give up hope—let nettles whet
The Sinking Man's *adieu* †

Poetry is when you pluck
A word from inner space,
Construing somehow *Friar Tuck*
Maid Marian's to chase †

Impassion'd fruit is on the vine,
As, falling hither south,
Its pips & pulp, in fine design,
Come drowning down my mouth †

Parting, sweet as honey's bet
On love to leave a stain,
Delicious daren't shun regret
Ecstatically sane †

Integrity's an empty thing
For escapees from truth—
As *crimson bulls will take to wing,*
To sugar-coat vermouth †

Beauty is a foreign tongue
I hadn't ever heard—
So sleek, so chic, unique & young,
As if her tonsils purr'd †

Love, of all the oddities
She kisses, to enact
Her leonine commodities,
Evolved—& *that's a fact* †

You want more food? Just purr the word!
Meowing, if you must
A quatrain nude—a thought occurr'd
To me: *In Garf we trust* †

Let *Sunshine* reign, let *Rain* pretend
It's coming, to be stopp'd—
As *Lilies of the Valley* spend
What sparklit Heavens dropp'd †

To be, or not to be at all,
As if you never were,
Will counter intuition, *Saul*
The butt of ev'ry purr †

Let *things of wood & stone* we chase
Leave divots in the sea
Of healing's grace—in second place
Insensitivity †

You have your hair, I have my heart—
We call it *compensation:*
I'd rather honey in my art
Than folly's poor relation †

Yeah, if you must, go label me
Follicularly challenged:
'Twould only serve t' enable me
To challenge, *who* is challenged †

Yep, *ego*, we go, is a word
To justify the end
Of insecurities, preferr'd
To minutes left to spend †

Another day, another day—
To which I will attest,
As hot *Apollo*'s golden rays
Diminish, *Daphne* blest †

Of ev'ry thought, my *Love-to-Be*
On fire, like a dove
For me, whose burning effigy
She cries on, from above †

You see, my dear, we coalesce:
You are so true & pure—
To hug me like a boa, press
Claws into lent allure †

Think nothing of it, *de rien,*
De nada, Monsignor:
Just sit there on your dunny-can—
Te amo, je t'adore †

To gaze into a soul so sweet
With reverential eyes,
Makes one, somehow so incomplete,
Her exponential prize †

If *hindsight* has its benefits,
Let *foresight* have its charms:
A word in order, when it fits,
Is putty in your palms †

Money talks, & honey walks,
But when she's here with me,
She's silky, savvy, sassy—*awks*
Am I: *four, one, two, three* †

If you go wrong, I went awry,
Beginning at the end—
For truth, for me, is but a spy,
On enigmatic trend †

I put a pretty penny down
Those willing pipes that wound
Your spirit-soul—too many drown,
Abandon'd & cocoon'd †

Peace is when you hear her jazz
Intone a gentle war
On silence—waves in *old La Paz*
Notes lapping on your shore †

A glamour puss, a sexy babe:
Creation's in-between
For *Adam, Abel, Aaron, Abe*—
& Pawns about to Queen †

Purrfection's when you can't improve
In artistry—to be
Her *joie de vivre*, in the *Louvre*
For *purrpetuity* †

A friend I wish I ever was
To thee, & him, & her;
Still you, so true, I woo, because
I wasn't, when you were †

The first few words of any line
Are written in my heart—
In blood & muscle, ink & wine,
& things that stick & start †

A sloth is very, very slow—
No affectation, true—
If *slothfulness* should ever go,
You'd be a kangaroo †

Shucks—Agaton, where did you go?
The shelves inside my mind
Are stacking, still, what stars bestow—
In esoteric kind †

Electric are the shoots & sharp
Ink recesses inclined
Eclectically—*play the harp*
(If only to unwind) †

Leave *Sphinx, my Lynx,* to love & rest,
Secure in my heart—
Since *Felis catus,* at her best,
Reposes in my art †

If love must reach equality,
I count on it to err:
For she is how my policy
May come up short—*to purr* †

Heiress apparent *(Ginger Rogers)*
Unto stardom's page,
Will whip up wile's wit, who dodges
One too farsome stage †

The Movie Star? She's moving well,
I thank you—to incur
Her groovy Pa, *three's two*, cling Belle's
High rank to *You-in-Fur* †

Tennis is a war, no less—
Regard the shooting stars:
Ego has no *pluralness*
For advertising cars †

Dogs eat dogs—if often frank—
Exhibiting their zeal's
Dank intent to walk the plank,
'Mid squawks, & squeaks, & squeals †

She is my *very best luck charm*,
My *fortune cookie's grove*—
Protecting all of me from harm,
When all the World's a stove †

For 1989's a year
In which I came to life,
Of fire born, to re-appear—
Lest Hades take a wife †

& on the 13th, of the 12th,
You saw the light of day:
To be *the Lamp of Love* yourself,
Descry delight's delay †

To see, or not to see—you see
The smiles & the hearts
Affected, not affecting thee
Envenom'd pens & darts †

Oft-times a pen is just a pen,
Cigars are just cigars:
A bold erection like *Big Ben*
Ain't *good* for many *bra*s †

Bizarre my *ideation?* May
You skeptics call it out:
The paranormal? Hey, betray
No room for doubts to doubt †

We walk, we talk, we go to school,
We live, & learn to love
The ones we leave, who aren't as cool—
If push'll come to shove †

It's like an open page, this screen
That beckons, & defends
What's yet to be, & what has been—
To fix quick what offends †

Enchantment truly knows no bounds,
Acquaintance thine to tether—
Not knowing thee sufficient, hounds
In tempests mine to weather †

Zounds! Forsooth, is that a word?
Let me try another:
Perhaps *purrfection* is *prefurr'd*—
If *cattery*'s a mother †

I'm calling time on wasting it
On soul-destroying trends:
I'm through with cut & pasting it—
To see how this one ends †

You speak in tongues? Try babble-ing
Like rivulets—aspire
To *polyglottal* dabble-ing
In *Mother Nature*'s choir †

Too average: Just hit a four,
Get out—each time you bat
A ton; to level up the score,
We'd smell a dirty rat †

Father Time & Mother Nature
Are, I hear, to wed:
They're just in time to hesitate,
Before we're put to bed †

A clash of egos—*this is war!*
They'll fight until one breaks
Up all inside—a quiet draw
Is more than winning takes †

Le Champion du Monde, alors,
Nous connaissons ton nom;
Un crocodile, il aime ton sort—
Pour n'être jamais con †

Le bout de tout est presque là—
Encore une fois tu gagnes—
À partir de ce moment va
Le doute: Chapeau, Montagne †

En français tu es héroïque,
En español el sol;
In English you play hide & seek—
To win *the Super Bowl* †

"Wie es Ihnen geht?" Ich ließ
"Ich frage mich" ja aus:
Er hat gelacht—"How are ya!" hieß
Die Antwort, ohne Paus' †

Des Himmels Günstling—der bin ich,
Der lebt allein mit mir,
Und ihr, die wie ein Licht entwich—
Und, nach wie vor, ist hier †

Papa's little Angel Possum,
Furry, purring Friend:
Never one for barkin', bossin'—
Loveliness on trend †

Barking dogs don't bite, they say,
Unless they're really both
Your *Canis vulpus,* here to stay
A little wolf—& wroth †

Who let the dogs out? Western stars
Bedevil black, as he
Confuses cars his bruising mars
For Eva's battery †

Of the notion, I was Hitler,
Disabuse did she:
As though Beethoven's hairy mitt
Stir circles in her sea †

Te amo, al fin del amor,
Mi corazón—en ti
Yo lo siento: por favor,
Contigo, ven a mi †

You are my she, she is my you,
&, when we are as one,
We will be they, they will be who
Knew loving has begun †

Bud, splutter butter on a page,
Indelibly delight—
As upper cutters, all the rage,
Majestically might †

Hearts aching, lest hers pine, to win
New sorrows, come what may,
Forsaking yester's wine, begin
Tomorrow's love, today †

He's what a curse rehearses? Then
Your sanity's at stake!
She's not averse to verses, when
Mortality's awake †

I'll hop it to *the Kennel,* Lads,
Lest, done Jacinta's tabs,
Guile cop it through the fennel pads—
Guest runner inta jabs †

I'd have to say I'm thinking—well,
Much better than before
They stuck two suckers' ends of gel,
& zapp'd *Tyrannosaur* †

Mancini knew a story grave,
Intoning it with notes
That, steering its *dénouement,* gave
Lachrymal overcoats †

A year or two, philosophizing,
Leads a man to love
Not only wisdom—*Levin* wising
Up, held *Kitty*'s glove †

So many books, so much to learn—
If only to be clear
That candlewicks are made to burn,
& books for holding near †

He gave me volumes priceless, tomes
To treasure, or be toss'd
Into the flames—as garden gnomes
Who rue tomorrows, moss'd †

A few *white lies,* just here & there,
Enough, to count the cost
*Adieu*s might prize, cuss dear & fair—
He's tougher found, than lost †

Ein paar Notlügen, hie und da—
Genügend, zu belehr'n,
Wie gut Adieus, im Singular,
Zerreißen und verzehr'n †

Mein Papa, Opa, Held, und Freund:
Sein Königreich gelangt,
Mir nachzuweisen, was mir säumt—
Und allen andern bangt †

Er hat, weiß Gott, Ihn bloß aus Irrtum,
Ja, umsonst erwähnt;
Denn auf der Erde herrscht Warrwirrtum—
Klar, wohin er sehnt †

For, lest the skies of honey seek
A better man than he,
Sure bless'd & wise let sunny speak
A letter's canopy †

What it is I want from you
Is what you want from me—
That is, if we were *Kathmandu,*
In *Key Biscayne*-to-be †

I throw away a word, or two,
Which soon becomes a line—
Whose wish to be a retinue
Of sentiments, is *thine* †

Ricco e famoso—non
La vita dolce fa:
Felice io sento con
La mia anima †

Im Schoß liegt sie, die kleine Katz',
Und hält Papa im Zaum—
Ihr nie und nimmer fehl am Platz,
Als wäre ich der Traum †

Sie ißt schon wieder aus der Schüssel,
Was ich ihr verteil;
Ihr Futter ist für sie der Schlüssel—
Millimeter geil †

Kannitverstan? In Amsterdam
They're waiting on *the GOAT:*
Auf seine Art ein Hamsterlamm—
Sich messend mit dem Tod †

Der liebe Gott, als wie bankrott,
Verleumdet und belacht,
Des Siegs Komplott flott ließ im Spott—
Des Diebes in der Nacht †

Who is John Galt? A somersault
Of logic to a choir:
So, what is it you think of him?
I don't—'cos I'm a liar †

Somebody laugh'd; somebody cried,
Like whistling in the wind
They call *Mariah*—open wide
To air-con, *Tamarind †*

La soirée qui vient
Ne reviendra plus:
Elle disparaît—rien
Ne vaut la peine, venu †

Rien à dire, rien à faire—
Ce qui vient, c'est l'avenir?
En plein été, donne-moi un verre
Du printemps, prêt-à-lire †

Les hommes se lancent, sans conséquences,
À fin de conquérir
Un ennemi, dans l'ignorance,
D'une âme—qui croie périr †

Let me give you riches, fame—
Your soul is all I ask;
Get thee to a prison, Jame,
Consolidate my task †

Impotent is God, who sends
Thee, winning, e'er to be
The way, in truth, of life that ends—
Beginning in the sea †